Living *in Gratitude Mode*

Your Passport to Abundance and Well-Being

Jeanette Salvatierra

DEDICATION

For my loves, my companions on this *Path*
forever and ever

Table of Contents

PREFACE

Always begin by being thankful. Be thankful for life, which is a journey filled with opportunities, some joyful, some painful, but all serving a purpose.

Whether we are believers or not, when we are grateful we activate positive energy that emanates from us, from within ourselves, to our surroundings. This energy, which some call vibration, friendliness, or charisma, connects us with higher levels of well-being, both physically and spiritually. Divinity, the universe, or whatever you call the superior entity that drives our creation, reactivates its beneficial power for each and every one of us who shows appreciation for the miracle of life.

How Do I Know? Firstly, because I've experienced it. Secondly, because my desire to understand the processes of the human experience, has led me to do research. And the wonderful part about research into gratitude is that the research and documentation come from scientists, mystics and even ordinary people like you and me.

However, as we are all unique beings and the expression of a totality that unites us as human beings, I decided to take a chance and write about my own experiences regarding gratitude.

My life experience is a combination of my own background and that of close relatives, friends and people I've met through my work as a life coach.

At first glance, we are all equal. At the same time, our lives are expression of a special uniqueness. That uniqueness stems from our choices. Under certain circumstances in life, each of us chooses our stance regarding circumstances, what options to explore or implement to resolve the problems we face, and what people we want to connect to for support, help or simply to accompany us.

It's based on our own choices that our lives differ. And when the choice we make is to be grateful for our circumstances, whatever they may be, we recharge our batteries with positive energy so as to be able to carry out actions that will enable us to overcome situations as best we can.

A Metaphor to Present My Story

Sight makes up 80% of our sensory experience. Meaning, we perceive life and the world around us primarily through our eyes. Sight is so paramount that in humans it's considered a driver and intensifier of sexual instinct: base for the reproduction and perpetuation of the species. That is why both men and women invest time in preening, and checking their image in the mirror, to attract potential sexual partners.

Therefore, for those interested in initiating courtship, everything from the educational system to entertainment focus their message on sight. We are primarily visual beings because we use our eyes to form our perceptions. But according to scientists, if we compare the senses and the keyboard of a piano, sight only represents the middle octave, 8 out of the 85 keys we can perceive as human beings. Of course sensory perception also includes our senses of hearing, smell, taste and touch, in addition to the sixth sense, or intuition.

Perception is composed of both the individual contributions of each sense and their summation.

In my research, I did not find actual percentages of such summations. It seems there are no concrete measures, as perception is a qualitative and subconscious process. But what's interesting is that nowadays the contributions of intuition in the perception process are acknowledged quite openly, though that may sound mystical or new age. In this book we will use the important concept of intuition to allow us to go further into the concept of gratitude.

When in 2003 I stopped driving my car because my failing vision made me a threat to myself and others, I had not heard about the relationship between sight and the middle octave of the piano. I simply felt limited, miserable, and perhaps punished for some forgotten sin. Or maybe it was just the worst luck in the world.

Twelve years later, and despite my having already accepted my lack of sight for a while, finding information about the wealth of perceptions from our "lesser" senses only reinforces my understanding that everything happens for a greater reason.

Thanks to my visual impairment, I've enriched my human experience, opening myself to sensations and activities that, before, were delegated to others or simply ignored.

For example, I have been able to care for my mother, pursue my dream of writing, spend quality time with my family and friends, connect with my intuition, and in general grow as a human being in service to others.

So, what better topic than that of gratitude for my first book? Anyway the first to be published, as I've had many writing projects in my inkwell for a while now.

My Offer to You

Through these pages I offer my life experience and my humble understanding of what gratitude can bring to your life.

I place at your disposal my effort to make this content simple, easy to implement, and flexible in its incorporation to your daily life. And I don't know if this is already clear to you, but gratitude should be a daily practice.

I offer you my sincere desire that this book inspires you so that, by activating gratitude, you may achieve greater abundance and well-being. That activation is what I call *living in gratitude mode*.

Thanks for the opportunity to share and grow together.

Jeanette Salvatierra-Barrios
Cooper City, Florida, 2015

ACKNOWLEDGEMENTS

My eternal thanks:

To *Jose and Andres Barrios* for your loving support and for serving as inspiration for many of my ideas.

To *my extended family*: my blood and my heart. May you all, whether physically present or not, receive my recognition and gratitude.

To *my friends* whose personal stories served as basis for the stories that exemplify many of the ideas of this book. While the names, situations and other personal details have been changed, the essence of their experience is present in these narratives.

To my teacher *Milagro Socorro* who took me under his wing when I decided to take the art of writing seriously.

And to my dear *Mariale Zabaleta* who with love and talent created the inner cover illustration.

To *Howard Goldberg* for the beautiful cover photograph

To *Jorge Luis Prado, Adriana Salvatierra, Loly Ferreiro, Carmen Cristina Wolf, Milagros Socorro and the Loly Graphics, Mincor and Creative Space* teams, for supporting me with the technical details of editing and production of this book.

INTRODUCTION

Over time I've learned that living in a perpetual attitude of gratitude is entirely possible. And very healing. A grateful attitude allows you to overcome challenges, make friends, be more productive and sleep better.

For many, gratitude is typically a sporadic expression to use in special occasions like birthdays or when receiving a gift or a form of recognition.

But my proposal is to make it a companion, a reinforcing factor of your personality and a tool for achieving success in life—just whatever your personal definition of success.

This companion, this attitude of gratitude, is what I call living in gratitude mode. So that you may experience the benefits of this way of living, I hope to support you in find gratitude in your everyday life.

Developing the Habit of Gratitude

To develop any habit and incorporate it in our daily lives, we must follow certain steps that have been verified as effective by hundreds of psychological studies, and reinforced by evidence from programs of eating well, meditating, and studying effectively, among dozens of other examples.

In this book we will incorporate this same method.

The formation of habits can be summed up in a three-step process. This book presents the elements necessary in each step of the process.

In Part One, I discuss the benefits of gratitude and the various elements involved, as well as cases or examples that illustrate these points.

In Part Two we provide an accompaniment so that you can develop the habit of gratitude. This we will do through a notebook or diary denoting three cycles of twenty-one days each. Every page should provide enough space to record the date and time of the exercise, as well as the *gifts of the day*. In addition, an original phrase or quote is offered with the aim of inspiring reflection.

Before the start of Part Two, I will provide more details about the purpose and intention of the notebook.

In the third part there will be information that will allow you, after the execution of the daily routine, to evaluate and deepen the benefits that gratitude provides.

I dare say this new routine will change the way you think and the way you see life.

Let's begin this wonderful journey toward an abundance of gifts and goods, to which gratitude is the ideal passport or safe-pass.

PART ONE: *Gratitude and Well-Being*

PART ONE

Chapter 1. An expression of love

G ratitude is a mechanism for people to appreciate what they have, instead of constantly thinking they need something new or in greater quantity to be happy. It's also a way to move away from the idea that they will not feel good until they succeed in satisfying all their material or physical needs.

Initially, gratitude may seem to some people like a dormant or limited ability. The good news is that gratitude can grow and be strengthened with practice.

Cultivating gratitude brings our awareness to the positive: the events and beings that make us feel love, joy, peace and all those nice feelings that we would like to propagate in our lives.

Further, when we express gratitude, i.e., write it or say it to others, gratitude creates an *atmosphere* of well-being that puts us in harmony with the environment.

That harmony between inner and outer is an expression of love. First toward our own lives, ourselves and our well-being. Second, it is an act of love toward others because the better we feel, the more helpful becomes our contribution to the well-being of those around us. And through our grateful interactions, positive connections reinforce and strengthen one another. As in any act of love, we are in an honest win-win situation inspired by the simple act of being grateful.

Furthermore, the attention we devote to being grateful gives us perspective on what is truly profound and what is mundane.

Simple things we take for granted or we don't even bother to notice. For example, the air you breathe, your parents' love, the support and complicity of an old friend, your child peacefully sleeping, your faithful pet, the colorful flowers in the park, and the mountaintop that decorates the horizon. Then there's the payment you receive for your work, the mammogram that comes back normal, the car that hasn't required a single repair in the past two years, and the lovely smile of the anchor person presenting the news that you happen to find appealing.

Simple things—important things, really—that we cannot pass by without being grateful for.

- Recurring things;
- Novel things;
- Things that (for now) you won't even discuss until they become realities.

If you haven't already, take a moment to:

- Mentally number the blessings you have to be grateful for, in each of the categories above;
- Be aware of the feelings you have just thinking about these things or people;
- Try to clearly distinguish each specific feeling in each case: joy, love, admiration, or acceptance.

Being aware of the positive feelings that come with being grateful, we begin to connect with the propelling energy of actions capable of bringing us closer to our goals, or to a superior state of physical well-being. Later we will explore the connection between gratitude and physical health.

Another perspective to consider is the role of gratitude as a key in discovering our purpose in life. By bringing attention to what happens to us, our personal relationships, our experiences with nature and our thoughts, we can recognize what we're passionate about.

Let's see how that works, through use of an example. Think for a moment about your current main activity (whether it is paid work or not). Whether you are a manager, an employee, whether you work for yourself or are a creator or a housewife, choose what is your main productive activity.

- Now identify another activity that you currently practice or that you would like to practice in the future. It could be something completely different or just a variation of your current occupation (for example: a specialization or a different company or workplace);

- Imagine the new job or activity. You can imagine the activities of an ordinary day, or the achievement of a goal related to your work; or see yourself interacting with other people in the workplace. Be grateful for this new task, position or career;

- Identify the intensity of the gratitude that each idea makes you feel;

- Compare the intensities.

Things we're passionate about, what really is our *calling* or our mission, are experienced more strongly. We appreciate with greater force or vehemence the gifts we like or love the most.

A Seeming Contradiction

So, what to do with negative experiences? In life not everything is always rosy. And in many cases we encounter an abundance of events or people that cause us fear, anguish, shame or disappointment. For those heartaches, gratitude can be a good remedy or tool for healing.

Being grateful even for those things that may at first seem negative. Above all, if it is not within our power to change things, we want to feel free of guilt, allowing us to learn life lessons with less pain.

Life offers pleasant events and happy times and also events that are negative or that cause us discomfort. This is a reality. We may see these discomforts as problems, difficulties that should not exist. But they are milestones along the path. They are circumstances, people or objects that are simply to be overcome.

When facing a problem or heartache, the first thought is usually: why me? If we adopt a more positive attitude, one originating in gratitude, our first thought becomes: What does this mean to me? Searching for meaning leads to exploring possibilities, beginning with an analysis that opens paths to overcoming our initial unrest. We move toward states of acceptance and even resolution, given the slightest possibility.

The point is to move from paralysis to action. As it is action that propels our transition toward success, a solution, or our acceptance of a condition that is not within our power to resolve. Even in this last case, we can identify scenarios where, even with an unresolved situation, we can pursue other goals and achieve well-being through new people or new situations.

An Example of Transformation and Gratitude

Danielle was diagnosed with a metastatic stomach, a cancerous condition. This was doubly painful news, as breast cancer had already caused removal of both her breasts three years prior. What did she do? This thirty-two-year-old woman decided to take positive action.

Danielle re-adopted the grateful attitude she had experienced when surviving her initial mastectomy. She focused her energy on ways to live a healthy life, believing that would make her new health challenge easier. She committed herself to attending the required periodic medical examinations, plus following a special diet. Danielle's additional mission was to motivate other cancer patients who were dealing with the same condition.

Danielle started a blog wherein she shared what she experienced and heard from other patients, and she gave talks to groups of family and friends. And every day she gave thanks for a life that allowed her to share information that helped people like herself.

Danielle's work began to gain notice through interviews with the media in her town. Today, more than ten years later, her condition is under control, she continues her motivational work, and she is a recognized author and lecturer in many English-speaking countries.

All this, according to Danielle herself, is due to gratitude and the transformation it caused in her, despite a condition that, for many, is totally adverse, and even deadly. Instead, Danielle's cancer became a new opportunity for success and well-being for her and those who knew her.

The key is to identify the opportunity. Despite the negative situation, we always have a chance to take positive action. We pause to evaluate, to feel and then think. Then we decide how to act in a way that allows us to take advantage of a situation that may have started out as very negative thus, justifying our initial gratitude.

Some Possible Reflections

Throughout this book you will find stories that exemplify the concepts being discussed. We invite you to read about each then pause to reflect on how that story reflects on a current situation in your life or in the lives of people in your environment. Ask yourself, how would I react in this case? What options do I have in my situation? What ideas, actions or feelings can I replicate in my personal circumstance?

In some stories, I will include specific questions. Other stories will be left open to your own analysis and interpretation.

The important thing is to take a moment to reflect on what the story induces in you.

Expressing Gratitude

Broadly speaking, human communication is composed of words and actions. So to express gratitude to someone, we can use phrases, gestures, verbal cues, written texts, images, drawings and many other forms of communication.

All this stems from an idea an intention within us—in the mind for the very rational; in the heart for the more emotional.

But without getting into the origin, the intention of gratitude, this remains true: if it is not expressed or shared, is incomplete. It's like someone waiting for the train to arrive, then once it arrives not getting on board. Or like the swimmer who arrives at the edge of the pool, then remembers he has something to do and never gets in the water.

Intention without action does not generate results.

In this chapter we try to encourage an intention of gratitude within you. Directly, through coaching questions that are listed, and indirectly through stories presented.

From that idea, thought or intention, we progressively move into action. In Part Two of this book, I offer a simple mechanism to begin to express gratitude, turning it into a daily practice until it becomes a habit, a recurring action that is almost automatic.

Repetition is the key to forming any habit and reinforcing it through achievements or rewards. In the case of gratitude, the benefits or rewards reveal themselves naturally. You feel more cheerful, optimistic and energized. In addition, the search for meanings in adverse situations will improve your creativity and confidence in your decision-making, to the extent that each new possibility will lead to your greater well-being.

In this digital age one might ask, why keep a hand-written diary? The answer is simple. Because it brings us back to our childhood, the point in our lives when we felt most creative and learned more easily.

Handwriting for adults, reactivates connections among brain cells, which when remaining dormant are the cause behind memory loss.

In addition, working with your hands, whether writing, drawing, or crafting, strengthens neuromuscular connections and improves eye-hand coordination (which increases the precision of movements and reduces the levels of mental and physical stress).

In the second part, this book offers sixty-three pages to be completed like a diary, i.e., three cycles of twenty-one days. Although many studies claim that with it takes twenty-one days of repeating a behavior for humans to make it into a habit, I wished to give my readers three opportunities.

In reality, each person may need more or fewer than twenty-one days. Providing sixty-three pages of diary is my way of honoring that possibility.

If for some reason, after having formed the habit of daily gratitude, you wish to resume the practice of writing by hand, if you like the diary format and want to reproduce it, or if you just want to read the sections or the Winds of Inspiration, the second part of the book facilitates that. That is my gift to you.

You can then keep your diary in your tablet, mobile phone or personal computer—or in whatever new medium is available at the time.

Express your gratitude in writing, and share it when you see fit. Or simply re-visit your thoughts from time to time.

Love is for sharing. If that love inspires gratitude, share the feeling with others. You will see it's worth it.

Chapter 2. Proof of Power

T he benefits that gratitude brings to those who express, experience, or come into contact with it, are various and have been scientifically documented.

I'm going to begin with scientific evidence validating the inner, or individual, benefits of gratitude. We will work our way toward evidence that supports those benefits in the areas of groups, organizations and community.

While I will not go into explicit detail of the studies, researchers and results, in the bibliography at the end of this book you will find those specifics.

I believe these studies and their results are extremely valuable. Not only do they rigorously use science to form and validate hypotheses, they also recognize the validity of observations of a more spiritual nature, which undeniably increase states of happiness, abundance and well-being.

On the other hand, the diversity of studies regarding gratitude, show us how powerful it can be as a tool for personal development.

Benefits for Our Personalities

Let's starting at the beginning: ourselves, our inner worlds, which then project our values, talents, emotions and intentions. Think of a house, the home of our being. We must first clean up the mess in our own houses, as our grandmothers might say, before we can clean up the mess in the world. This makes us more capable of receiving opportunities for wellbeing and abundance.

Happiness

Gratitude increases the levels of happiness of those who experience it. In one of the fundamental studies of positive psychology concerning happiness and its causes, they found that all participants, regardless of age, gender, academic level or even physical health, showed an improvement in mood, optimism and energy after experiencing gratitude.

In cases of people with chronic or disabling disease, for example, the daily practice of counting blessings and expressing gratitude for them, when sustained for twenty-one days, improved levels of energy. The subjects became more positive, their interactions with others improved, and their levels of acceptance of their conditions, increased, resulting in improved moods and happiness levels.

From my personal experiences and my participation in support groups for people with visual disabilities and chronic diseases like diabetes and cancer, I can testify as to the benefits of gratitude on both individuals and groups. It not only improves the general attitude one has toward the life they're living but also strengthens empathy and group cohesion.

In studies with adolescents and young adults, participants who gathered at least three times a week to say thanks, were found to display greater joy and fewer negative emotions and violent episodes than those who did not regularly gather to say thanks.

These result show that you are never too young to begin a practice of gratitude, and the earlier in life we learn to be grateful, the sooner we will experience joy, and the longer it will last. The challenge for us parents, is to teach our children the practice of gratitude early in life.

As with many of the teachings parents pass down to their children, gratitude is taught by example. Some ideas I suggest bringing into practice are the following:

- **Being grateful daily:** for example, before a family meal; before leaving home for an important event (a child's game, play or dance); at the end of the day, before sleeping, or before or after any important moment with your family;

- **Family traditions and rituals:** expressing gratitude on important dates for the family; for example, birthdays and anniversaries. This not only demonstrates and encourages gratitude but also helps to strengthen family ties, generating memories that define human connections for children and teenagers, and thus the foundations of the personality of healthy adults. Gratitude can be expressed through giving small gifts, the preparation of a special dish, lighting candles, releasing sky lanterns, or any other special activity, explaining to children that those events are a display of gratitude;

- **Experience and simulations:** we can take a family trip to a place nearby or in another country, helping out in a low-income community. Learn of others' living conditions, sharing in their meals and chores, permits children to value the comforts they enjoy in their homes. This activity is ideal for older children and teenagers. Another idea is to limit the luggage brought along, to accentuate the lack of material goods that may exist in the destination visited;

- **Organization of activities of service:** collecting toys in good condition, food, school or home supplies, or money, and donating it to an institution for people in need. Or your children can take the donations and deliver them personally to the beneficiaries. This activity teaches not only gratitude but also solidarity and empathy;

- **Metaphors and symbols:** using them to teach gratitude in challenging or adverse situations. For example, if a child does not pass a school exam, a favorite book or television character can be used to relive that moment and declare the lesson learned ("I must pay attention in class," for instance, or "I will study more or practice solving more math problems"). Invite the child to be grateful for what the character learned from that situation. Using symbols to express gratitude could be offering a grandmother tickets for having taken care of the children, or it could be wearing an item to express gratitude, such as a medal for a baseball victory, or a bracelet or ribbon in gratitude for the recovery of an ill loved one.

It is important to emphasize, especially when it comes to children's education, that it is not about expressing gratitude through religious dogma, unless of course one is religious.

If you're religious and usually thank God, and you wish to transmit your beliefs to your children, try using these suggestions. But if not, no problem. There are many ways to express gratitude in a family moment observed in harmony and in healthy conditions.

To conclude, I would like to refer to the results of a study that reinforces the importance of gratitude in children. According to this study, children who practice gratitude have a better attitude toward their families and school work. So incorporating gratitude practices between their house chores can yield good results in the short, medium and long term.

Self-Esteem

Many therapies aim to improve self-esteem through positive affirmations to induce appreciation of our personal qualities.

"I'm talented," we might say, or, "Others consider me attractive, intelligent and loving because I am." The next step: after recognizing the quality or ability, one should feel gratitude for it.

It is not about promoting a narcissistic personality or inflating our egos. It is about expressing gratitude for positive personal characteristics, and continuing to exploit them in service to a healthy relationship or partnership in our professional field, as well as in our city or community.

On the other hand, demonstrating our talents gives us the opportunity to share them, progressively becoming less egocentric and selfish.

So gratitude can prompt us to invest in people that are less fortunate or lacking the qualities or skills we have.

Gratitude creates a balance between raising self-esteem and reducing selfishness. I particularly believe this balance is not only more positive but also more realistic.

To experience the benefits of gratitude in your own self-esteem, I suggest the following exercise:

- Begin by finding a quiet place where you feel comfortable and will not be interrupted for fifteen to twenty minutes;

- If you wish to record your ideas with pencil and paper, or with a voice recorder, you may do so. This will allow you to revisit your conclusions when you feel it necessary;

- Take three deep breaths through your nose. Relax your body and focus your attention on your breathing;

- Notice, feel, and think about those talents or attributes you possess that you think are positive, and for which you feel grateful. These attributes might be physical (for example, the color of your eyes or the strength of your legs); emotional (for example, your compassion toward others or your joviality); or your personality (tenacity, patience or knowledge);

- Think, write or say aloud, "I am thankful for this quality I've identified."

This exercise of identifying and affirming good qualities then being grateful, improves self-esteem. This can also make it easier to choose a talent to develop for serving others, something that promotes well-being in ourselves through the well-being of those in our environment.

Optimism

When we look at the world through the lens of gratitude, our stance is more open and, thus, we can experience future circumstances with more optimism.

This is a scientific fact proven by a study conducted on chronically ill people who were asked to keep journals. When asked about their expectations the following week, those who had practiced gratitude were found to be more optimistic than those who did not.

Their optimism was even found to be contagious to those

around them. In that same study, the wives of grateful participants reported an increase in optimism in their acceptance of the status of their spouses.

Several studies have shown an inverse correlation between depression and gratitude. In other words, the more grateful you feel, the less depressed you'll be.

Once we see optimism as the opposite of depression, we can systematically avoid the latter through practice of gratitude.

Spirituality

Gratitude is directly correlated with spirituality. It is unclear if one is more spiritual for expressing gratitude (as proposed by many religious practices), or if one is more grateful when one is more spiritual due to feeling a connection to a supreme entity or force.

What is certain is that gratitude, by making us focus on more important things, leads us to more transcendent positions, more occupied with the intangible elements of life, such as emotions and our personality, and giving less attention to material aspect.

A very interesting discovery was reported by a study on materialism and happiness. The conclusion, probably obvious to many of us, is that material goods and excessive consumerism do not lead to happiness.

Among people who were poor or had low incomes, it was found that in 70% of individuals happiness was linked to the possession of material goods. However, people who were more economically fortunate did not experience higher levels of happiness. What's more, the greater the material wealth, the unhappier people were. It seems that people become desensitized to material possessions as their quantity increases (the effect of hedonic adaptation), to the point of no longer appreciating what they have.

However, when people, regardless of their income levels, do not focus on what is material yet are appreciative of it, not only do they report higher levels of satisfaction with their lives, but their confidence in their divine connection improves, as well. In other words, they become more spiritual.

Impact on Emotions

Our emotions reflect the responses of our mind and body to the events we live. If gratitude is present in our thoughts, many of those emotions will be of a pleasant nature. Better, given that our feelings affect our health and well-being in general, it turns out to be economically attractive to invest in gratitude. We receive more than one benefit for one simple effort.

Test it out for yourself. Try to identify the specific emotion experienced by being grateful for something. I think you'll find that in every case the emotions are in the spectrum of the positive: joy, pleasure, peace. These are only a few examples. You will surely discover many more.

Reduced Stress

By expressing gratitude and elevating our levels of happiness, we ease the tension caused by external shocks and concerns.

Of course we want to express genuine appreciation for real benefits. It is not about self-denial, or denying the existence of a negative person. It is about being honest, acknowledging the good that is present in our lives, even if it is something very basic, like the air we breathe, or perhaps something more complex, that requires effort and dedication to achieve.

Gratitude inspired by genuine positive aspects of our lives, reduces, and can even eliminate, stress caused by whatever is not going as well as we'd like.

And I mean excess stress, because there is always stress. That can never, nor should it be, completely eliminated because it is part of our instinct of alert, compelling us to act quickly when in imminent danger.

Gratitude is not a sedative or an anesthetic. It's a positive and calming energy. Gratitude is the energy of balance.

One day my son, then eight years old, asked me why I was always so sad and nervous about not being able to see well. I had to explain that several doctors, in four different countries, agreed that I was losing my sight little by little and would eventually be completely blind. That diagnosis, I explained, made me nervous and cranky, because it made me feel like I wouldn't be able to continue to enjoy my life, my family and my career. My child looked at me and very seriously asked, "Mom, but does that it mean you're going to die?" I immediately replied no, to which he replied, "Well then, Mommy, don't be nervous. You should be grateful that you get to keep living."

Not only did I find his profound but simple wisdom astounding, I also understood what was really important, what I could truly feel grateful for: that I would get to continue to enjoy my son, with or without my vision.

Certainly, I have relaxed. And every time I feel stressed about not being able to do something because of my limitations, I remember my son and give thanks for being alive. And relax even more!

Increased Adaptability

Gratitude makes us more flexible. It allows us to adapt better and more rapidly to changing or unknown circumstances.

Everything from the opportunity to live new experiences, to the confidence founded on belief in a higher entity. Gratitude opens the mind to change and transformation without resistance or pain.

There's a story I always use to illustrate this point:

The F. family had everything to feel grateful and happy about while living in their country of origin. A twenty-something year-old couple who were in love and worked as a team, had three healthy children, a job, their own home, cars, travel, and education. But when the economic and political situation in their country changed for the worse, they were forced to emigrate.

The husband found a job in a company in his area of expertise, but the wife had to close her business and devote herself to being a housewife. They move to a new country, lived for two years in a small rented house. The children went from a private school to a public school, which, despite their excellent academic quality, were over-populated, resulting in the social groups being more competitive and somewhat aggressive.

Still, the F. family often expressed how grateful they were for the change, which provided them in a new life experience, a new culture, a new language, plus personal and economic security.

The adaptation of the family to new circumstances was fast and without trauma, all facilitated by gratitude.

In addition, it has been found that grateful people overcome the grieving process more easily and are more capable of accepting help and recovering from the obstacles that come with change.

Reduced Feelings of Envy

In appreciating the good that we have in our lives, we improve our self-esteem and confidence, reducing our tendency to compare ourselves to others and feel envious of their possessions or qualities.

It may sound somewhat innocent or too altruistic, but the reality is that gratitude makes us dig so deeply into what we value and what makes us happy; it leads us to recognize that we cannot know how happy another person is based only on what they allow us to see of their personalities, lives and values.

In other words, gratitude helps us understand that *not everything that glitters is gold*, and so, feeling envious of others would be like longing for a mirage.

Facilitating the Memory of Good Times

According to psychologists, people tend to remember things in a distorted manner unless they make a conscious effort to record things just as they happen. In particular, negative events may be stored in our memories as though they were worse or more traumatic than in reality.

By practicing gratitude in the present moment, we record in our memories events as they occurred, so that when we subsequently evoke these pleasant and positive recollections, they will be stronger and more realistic.

Gratitude can also be used as a mechanism for overcoming grieving. A practice that has recently become popular is the celebration of someone's life, to replace the classic mournful funeral. At these events, which may or may not contain elements belonging to the religion of the deceased, family and friends remember personal characteristics and fond moments, and share poems, music and even meals that would please the deceased.

These reminders or celebrations of life allow survivors to show their gratitude for the life and contributions of the dearly departed, facilitating natural grieving.

The Effects of Gratitude on Health

Gratitude has been widely studied by doctors and psychologists, as an element to incorporate into therapies for pain management in chronic or terminal illnesses, and as a mechanism of prevention.

In the United States, medical schools of major universities such as Harvard, plus hospitals and research centers such as Cleveland Clinic incorporate gratitude in their practices. This is also encouraged in the general public through print, electronic newsletters and blogs.

While it is true that no direct link has been found between expressing gratitude and curing serious diseases, there are improved moods and states of mind among patients who practice gratitude regularly. Gratitude makes them more receptive and optimistic about their situation, facilitating the treatment process.

Let's look in detail at some results of research done when gratitude interventions were incorporated into treatment and prevention protocols.

Improvements in Sleep

The practice of writing in a gratitude journal before bedtime, or mentally going over the events of the day that inspire gratitude, facilitates relaxation, allowing for a deep and restful sleep.

The effect of sleep on mental and physical health has been verified in numerous studies and is clear through mere observation. Sleeping facilitates cellular regeneration and is key to keep the brain working efficiently, helping us maintain mental clarity and stability.

In my personal experience, going over my gratitude list at the end of the day helps me fall asleep more quickly. It's what I like to call "slowing down the mental motor." This creates a state of relaxation that lasts the whole night. Try it and in few days' time you will thank me for this recommendation!

Increased Physical Exercise

People who practice gratitude regularly tend to exercise more often than others. This fact was documented in the first decade of the 21st century by a study conducted in the United States by two researchers at prestigious universities.

This study divided people into three groups that recorded in a journal one of three different types of circumstances: circumstances they were grateful for, situations they worried about, and situations in general without judging them as positive or negative.

Participants in the "grateful" group reported exercising an average 1.5 hours longer than "worriers." In addition, the grateful group reported fewer health complaints than the rest of the participants in the study.

Longevity

While there is no specific study that has shown grateful people to live longer, if we check all the emotional, mental and physical benefits of gratitude, we can very probably come to the conclusion that the practice of gratitude can lengthen life.

Additionally, extrapolating the benefits of gratitude from occupational and social perspectives, grateful people tend to experience positive economic conditions, interpersonal relationships and community relations. All are in a position to live longer, to prosper more, and to enjoy healthy communities.

Professional Benefits

Gratitude has proven to be a powerful tool in the improvement of the working environment, resulting in motivated employees and contributing to a positive organizational culture for employees, businesses, clients and the community in general.

Let's see in detail some of the benefits of gratitude.

Staff Motivation

Instilled properly by supervisors and managers, the expression of gratitude for contributions by partners and employees can be a motivating element, as potent as salary or bonuses.

In addition to its low cost, gratitude can be effective immediately. There is no need to wait for end of month or fiscal year to reward an employee's achievements, productivity or client satisfaction with an act of gratitude. Whatever the reason, the immediate supervisor can thank an employee in person, with a simple email, or by other means at his or her fingertips.

From my years of corporate life, I have particularly fond memories as an employee and as a manager, of the regular practice in my sales department of ringing the sales bell.

At the entrance of the sales manager's office, we had installed a bronze bell which was only rung when a major contract was signed. No matter the amount—it could be a couple hundred dollars or a million—that bell was sounded. The importance was let the amount than the client, the complexity of the competitive situation, the type of product or innovation that it represented in the market, or the amount of resources and time involved in the contract.

Once the seller arrived at the office, he or she would find the manager waiting, and they would ring the bell together. Immediately, the whole staff on the floor would go to the office to hear the news, the congratulations, and the manager's thanks to the sales team.

This simple ceremony not only motivated the acknowledged seller, it encouraged the other salespeople.

The effect of gratitude was proven by researchers who found that, in the United States, about 66% of employees felt low motivation as a result of not receiving expressions of gratitude from their supervisors or employers.

So, the gratitude of the company expressed by managers and supervisors, is valuable as a motivating factor on a level with more tangible elements such as bonuses and promotions.

Teamwork

In any organization, the complexity of the tasks and the level of expertise of the people required leads to establishment of working groups or teams.

Talent, knowledge, and technical expertise alone are not enough for a team to be successful. The relationship among members also forms an important part of the factors that contribute to success.

If relationships in the team are characterized by mutual appreciation, people will work with more dedication and attention to detail, and often exceed goals and expectations. This represents not only a positive impact on the working environment, but also leads to higher productivity.

The Organizational Health Index is a measurement of the level of satisfaction of employees within a particular team. In some businesses such as consulting services, this index is used to compensate team leaders. One of the components of the index relates to the capacity of the leader to recognize, and express gratitude for, the contributions of team members.

In the index measurements of a well-known international business, between the years 1999 and 2009 they found that in teams wherein the members were thanked for their contributions, the index showed higher values than that of team members not systematically thanked.

Development of Professional Connections

Gratitude can be fertile ground to cultivate and develop networks of professional relationships.

For example, thanking those who teach us through their trajectory, helps to strengthen the relationship between a professional and potential mentors. Similarly, expressing gratitude among colleagues for help received, or for a job well done that facilitates the work itself, can foster relationships of trust, respect and even friendship, all of which can be beneficial in the future.

If you wish to participate in a mentoring process in your company, or even develop a sponsorship in your professional field, begin by identifying a person with greater experience than you, whose success is similar to your own career goals. Make the most of routine interactions in your organization such as meetings, training sessions or chats, to express gratitude to your potential mentor for his or her example and achievements. As well, a virtual relationship can be established with a professional you don't know by subscribing to his or her website or blog, or following social networks. Be sure to express gratitude in your comments and share his or her tweets or posts, or better yet, eventually write a personal email expressing gratitude and offering that leader information that may be valuable in return.

That way, if you wish to request that person be a mentor or sponsor, you will already have developed a relationship or connection based on gratitude.

Gratitude and Our Relationships

As noted by several researchers, gratitude has amazing benefits on our physical and psychosocial health.

Specifically, in our relationships with our partners, family and close friends, gratitude strengthens these relationships over time if regularly expressed.

Gratitude makes us nicer.

The positive effects of gratitude on our states of mind, our humility, and our self-esteem, turn us into people who attract others, who then attract others with whom we can interact readily.

Nobody likes to deal with someone cranky, arrogant or envious. Gratitude progressively *dissolves* these negative characteristics, as mentioned in this chapter.

Greater Social Acceptance

In two studies conducted with 243 people, individuals who regularly practiced gratitude obtained 17.5% greater social acceptance compared to those who did not.

In other words, if we are grateful, people tend to like us more. That high percentage of acceptance is what is known as social capital.

One might well wonder what his or her social capital is. The numerical result is not relevant. Simply observe how your immediate interpersonal relations express how people feel about your way of being. The mechanism of improvement is simple: be more grateful to your loved ones, friends and the people you see frequently such as public servants, nurses and sales people.

Better and More Lasting Relationships

Does it surprise you that gratitude leads to better relationships? Expressing appreciation for the qualities of your partner, is essential for a stable and happy relationship.

After observing and dealing with marriages for more than two decades, researchers have determined that, unless a partner maintained a relationship of five-to-one or higher between their positive and negative interactions, the union was doomed to fail and come to an end.

In other words, for every complaint or expression of anger, you must generate at least five positive expressions such as compliments, smiles, thank-you's or jokes, or trouble lies ahead.

So if you have a partner, whether you are married or not, take these findings into account and avoid entering a failed statistic. For this, you have gratitude as an ally.

Throughout this chapter, I've submitted results from major studies on the benefits of gratitude, as well as some true stories, a few reflection exercises, and particular cases.

I hope to have convinced you, but above all, I hope to have motivated you to practice gratitude regularly. The change you will experience in your life will, I'm sure, be so positive that you will find even more reasons to be grateful.

Let us be grateful for gratitude's beneficial power.

Chapter 3. Gratitude and Abundance: Some Real-Life Examples

T he question that follows, a rhetorical one no less, is along the lines of the chicken or the egg and applies to the matter of gratitude and abundance.

What comes first? Being grateful for the abundance that surrounds us? Or being grateful without seemingly enjoying any abundance? Or maybe being abundantly grateful to attract an activity that will bring us abundance?

The interesting thing is that all the above scenarios are valid. But he or she who is truly powerful will begin by feeling selfless gratitude. It seems like a contradiction, but to achieve something, we must first do nothing.

Well, nothing specific. The first action to take is to express gratitude for the expected result.

To be grateful from absolute trust is an achievement of the focus that I strongly propose. A combination of rational approaches: positive psychology, coaching and spirituality. I must admit, in this case, the order of the factors does alter the product.

Addressing the relationship between gratitude and abundance, calls primarily for a spiritual approach followed by a rational one. To express any idea in the material world, first we must want it and strengthen that desire with confidence born in the spirit.

Absolutely everything that exists was imagined some time before. It is therefore natural to show gratitude from the beginning. Just conceive the idea and formulate the intention that appropriate action will produce the result. No matter the amount of effort, the number of attempts, or adjustments to the original idea, this remains true. Gratitude is what boosts the initiation of the creative process, and the result is amplified in quality and quantity. Meaning, abundance.

Abundance and Prosperity

Abundance suggests as great quantity of goods or other things, quantities that satisfy our desires or needs.

Prosperity is understood as the enjoyment of abundance. This concept also relates, thanks to advertising and marketing in general, with the material aspects of life: money, luxury, cars and so on.

However, both abundance and prosperity can be applied in much broader ways, to refer to non-material aspects of human existence. In this way, we enhance the totality, not just a part.

Attracting abundance and prosperity can work together, as both include the intangible, subtle and eternal, as well as the material, tangible and concrete. As in life itself, achieving abundance and prosperity contributes to our happiness and well-being.

From this broadened perspective, we can see that we all are abundant. If we devote our attention for a moment to the essential circumstances of our lives, we always find an element of abundance.

Several examples:

- The number of cells in our body, each one different and specialized to perform a certain function that give life to the body;

- Our life experiences that teach us to appreciate each other and

46

ourselves;

- The brain and its almost infinite capacity to create and learn;

- Feelings, both the positive and negative;

- Breathing, which allows us to continue living.

If we look around us, we also find multiple examples of abundance:

- The light and heat of the sun;

- The water that falls as rain and the air around us;

- The various useful things from the land, as well as those processed and bought at the market;

- The different expressions on the faces of passers-by on the street;

- The joy of children or pets that walk by.

The first list is composed of specific inner aspects; the second list contains examples of external abundance. In both cases, the list can be much longer, and neither list refers to material possessions.

The idea is to invite you to recognize abundance from a broader perspective.

Take a moment to reflect on the abundance in your life today. Anything on a personal, inner, individual level, plus those in your daily environment and relationships.

It is possible that during this exercise you are confronted with aspects that are not very positive or that cause you unhappiness and frustration. These aspects, if abundant, are also part of your list. Do not be surprised. For now, simply add them. If you're making your list on paper, put the abundantly negative elements in one column and in another column list the abundantly positive.

The Good, the Bad and the Doubtful

At this stage of the exercise, you probably have in your head or on paper a table of two rows (inner aspects, outer aspects) and two columns (positive things, negative things). We'll call this the Table of Aspects.

	Positive things	Negative things
Inner aspects		
Outer aspects		

As you realize the abundance in your life, some aspects may seem of ambiguous nature; i.e., we are not sure if they are good or bad at first sight.

For example:

- Having a lot of hair;
- Muscle pain after exercising;
- The noise produced by the musical practice of your child or neighbor;
- The amount of morning traffic when we go to work.

At first, sort these aspects as you wish, but mark them with an asterisk or some other kind of symbol. Then come back to them.

Careful analysis of these *ambiguous* aspects exercises our creativity and reduces the stress of uncertainty.

Being Grateful for What?

We can easily be grateful for the good and the positive in our lives, no matter how little or how much. And if the positive is abundant, even better.

But we can be grateful for the negative? Contrary to our initial reaction, the answer is yes.

When we recognize that first and foremost, the negative aspects simply form part of our existence, of being alive and being able to experience them is reason enough to be grateful. Accepting does not mean embracing something, inviting it to remain. We don't intend to live in discomfort, sadness or lack. I mean, at first, don't resist it. We don't want to increase our current discomfort by going against the current, which can paralyze us with sadness or masochistic suffering.

I mean we simply realize that something is there, whether it is due to our conscious action or not.

When one is confronted by the presence of the negative, one might ask him or herself:

1. What good is this going to do for me? What can I learn from this?
2. Is it possible to actively transform the negative into positive?
3. If I can't change it, how do I coexist with this negative thing in my life?

These questions open up an active, more powerful perspective. Answering these questions can begin a transformation in us, a change in our perception of negative circumstances that can lead us to a solution. In other words, we get closer to well-being.

In fact, by changing our perspective, we might be able to find how to be grateful for something that we previously thought negative. The power to learn from the negative, to define and implement a plan to make it positive, constitutes a valid reason to be grateful.

Before continuing, please return to your lists and analyze the events marked as negative or ambiguous, applying the three questions of transformation.

Observing a Fact from Two Perspectives

I heard this story from one of my coaching teachers at an event a while back.

My teacher, whom I will call Julia, was being driven to an event by her colleague Lucas who had offered to drive her there. At one point, traffic became haltingly slow, threatening the possibility of their arriving at their destination on time.

Lucas began to be tense, complaining about the number of cars, the lack of skill of the drivers, the overheating engine, and pretty much anything and everything. Julia, who was not driving, spent that time enjoying the sky, being grateful for how clear and unclouded it was, and curiously observing driver's facial expressions. Julia appreciating the various car models and so on, completely forgetting that she might be late to her appointment.

A few minutes later, Lucas and Julia saw that the reason for the heavy traffic was an accident involving several vehicles attempting to enter a crowded parking lot. With this new knowledge, both Lucas and Julia breathed a sigh of relief and experienced gratitude

This story demonstrates two applications of gratitude. Can you identify them??

Gratitude helps us maintain a state of calmness and appreciation. And it helps to understand and accept the outcome of what seems a valueless conflict.

Another Story to Reflect On

Derek is twenty-nine years old. He and his twenty-five-year-old wife Pat just had their first baby, Peter. The three are a close young family. However, Derek will not get to see his son grow up because he has a congenital condition called Retinitis Pigmentosa, which progressively leaves a person blind.

Despite this, Derek considers himself very lucky. He graduated with honors in Computer Science, he has a job that challenges him and that pays well. He is head of systems in an organization dedicated to the education of children and adults with visual disabilities. He frequently participates in consulting and evaluation of software products dedicated to those with impaired vision. Now totally blind, Derek has a keen sense of humor, he can communicate in several languages, and he plays bass guitar in a rock band that he's been in since he was a teenager.

"Many people feel sorry for me when they see me so young, walking with my guide dog," he says, smiling. "But once they get to know me and they see that I am like any other man my age, their compassion is often transformed into admiration and extra support for me. I have achieved many of my goals, thanks to the support I receive from others. And I don't think it's pity. I like to think that I inspire them to help me."

This is because Derek is a grateful person, despite his serious physical limitation, he has succeeded in various ways.

Some questions to reflect on

1. Is Derek's attitude toward life appropriate?

2. Do you think that his is a valid attitude in any circumstance, even if one has a very limiting condition?

3. Would Derek have the same opportunities to be an example if he had some lesser condition?

There is no right or wrong answer. But as they say, "It is better to inspire others than to pity the constraints we may have."

Returning to the Rhetorical Question

From what was discussed so far in this chapter, we can conclude that gratitude makes no distinction between what our rationality considers good or bad. Being grateful for something we initially thought negative is always possible. Just by transforming our perception, we can consider a negative event an opportunity to learn and create new circumstances.

But this gratitude comes after the fact. The most powerful thing is to be grateful before experiencing the event.

Reaping What You Sow

Throughout my life, I have emphasized the importance of preparing before any activity. Preparation puts us in an advantageous position for achieving our objectives or goals.

And I don't mean just the classic examples of studying for a test or a speech in front of an important audience.

I also mean preparing myself for simple daily activities. For example, I prepare to go to the dentist or the doctor by listening to my favorite music, having a cup of tea or doing something else relaxing or calming. If I want to find a good place where my driver can park the car, I suggest finding a less congested parking lot beforehand, appreciating the fact that a longer walk is good and necessary exercise.

Preparing beforehand not only encourages a positive result but also creates within us a positive attitude, and we feel more relaxed about the situation.

Let's look at this idea in detail. First of all, preparation puts us in a state of openness, acceptance and peace. Next, our inner state is reflected in our outer attitude, which is actually what the world outside of us, experiences and responds to.

Outer responses are a reflection of our own attitude. In other words, external interactions are of the same class or frequency as the internal.

Therefore, a positive outcome is virtually guaranteed when we prepare and assume a positive and winning attitude beforehand. So, without a doubt, we can thank the result even without yet experiencing it because we are preparing the ground and planting the seed.

Our gratitude can be very intense, depending on how much we trust the outcome. Since the external response is always influenced by our inner attitude, abundance too is a result of our inner state, our gratitude.

Now, I am not telling you this to sound irrational or naive. I am simply asking you to be generally positive, to take on an open, relaxed attitude that contributes to your general well-being, as we have discussed in previous chapters.

And do not blindly take my word for it. Put these tools into practice. Experience gratitude in your own life and see its value. The experience will be worth it.

If we cultivate positivity through our intentions and preparations, the results we want are those we achieve. And they are always abundant.

Liberating Options

Sometimes, even after the best and most consciously positive preparations, the results are not what we expect. Things can go wrong. But even so, there are options and solutions.

Keep an open and positive attitude, even when the results are slow in coming. Try applying the three questions of transformation. Other possible solutions will most likely appear when a new plan of action is developed.

A positive attitude while we reboot assures us of more creativity in ideas and progress toward our objectives and goals—and, in addition, can motivate the support and cooperation of other people to facilitate our actions.

We must remember that we are not alone. Unless you live in an island in the middle of the ocean, or in a hidden cave on a remote mountain, other people can spontaneously conjoin their energy with our actions, but we must attract them with our positive energy.

The decisions we make after a failure are ours to make. We can either let ourselves dwell on not obtaining our goal, or we can free ourselves of guilt and negativity and continue to look within and listen to our dreams, considering novel pans of action, and finding ways to see the good in our initial failure.

Let us stop here for a bit to analyze this thing *failure*.

When the results of our actions are not as expected, or simply when circumstances change disadvantageously, we typically feel discomfort, rejection, shame or pain.

This initial shock of disappointment is natural, and as such, we must accept and live with it. What I mean by this is that there is no reason to run away from feeling bad, or sad, or in pain because of a situation in life. Take the time to feel your discomfort and ready yourself to move to the next step or stage of your life.

What we cannot do is remain stagnant, allowing our pain to become suffering. If we do, not only does our physical and mental health deteriorate, which can result in depression and worse, but we distance ourselves from possible solutions, chances to improve ourselves, and potentially important and positive people in our lives.

Once I heard that the failure is nothing more than a call to resume our true path as planned out by God, the universe or fate—however you wish to refer to the creator or supreme energy. I have witnessed many cases of failure to achieve success that have led to exactly the right adjustment and eventual triumph. Success is not only defined as a visible achievement, but also as the return to one's true calling, passion or purpose in life.

Failure, or Returning to the True Path?

Luis wanted to study medicine but, despite his excellent grades, he was not accepted to the main medical school in his country. So he took his second option, going to a chemical engineering school with hopes of eventually transferring to medicine.

But math, geometry, and engineering, were not his forte. At the end of the second semester, Luis's GPA was so low, he could only see his college experience as an uphill battle.

Luis became despondent, lost weight and abandoned his interest in sports and drawing, activities he had practiced since childhood and enjoyed very much.

That summer, he returned home and announced his decision to leave college. He felt he had failed, and his shame was so great he could not figure out how to move forward.

One afternoon, while talking with a friend who attended a private university in the capital, Luis learned that the university had two years earlier opened a school of dentistry. Given that it was private school, the admission process was different and would not be affected by Luis's current academic situation.

Luis investigated all the requirements and costs, requested help from his parents, and in September began his studies in dentistry.

This story occurred twenty-two years ago. Luis not only graduated but discovered his passion for Pediatric Dentistry. He now has two patents in dental surgery instrument and has published two books. One of his books is about tooth care for children, illustrated by himself. Luis's practice combines his lucrative private practice and quality care for low-income children in a hospital of the Adventist faith. This is what happens when "failure" is followed by re-examination of options and positive action.

Some Questions to Reflect On

1. What similar circumstances of apparent failure have you experienced in your life?

2. How did you react in the moment? What people, ideas or alternative actions did you take?

3. What would you do differently today, using gratitude as an element of analysis or action? (Hint: implement the three questions of transformation.)

4. What new approach could you take for a similar situation you are currently experiencing?

When we take one course of action and do not attain our goal, we can simply choose another course of action. As this happens we experience various emotions and put into practice different ideas, comparing and collaborating with other people. And we can continue forward, grateful for the experience and powered by confidence that we will eventually achieve our goals and dreams.

Living in Gratitude Mode

The daily practice of gratitude, as it best suits our current context, puts us in a mental and physical attitude that promotes well-being. In addition, having confidence in the power of our intention and our action ideas, puts us on track for achieving abundant results.

This way of living, of experiencing situations of our daily life, is what I call *living in Gratitude Mode.*

Gratitude based on the certainty that the future will be rich in blessings.

As a child I was fascinated by stories about the future, life in space and intergalactic exploration. In my favorite futuristic movies, after the good guys prepared themselves for their dangerous journey, the real excitement began with the countdown to the moment the big red button would launch the ship into an adventure filled with lessons and achievements.

Once the trip had begun, I noticed, everything changed. Nothing in space resembled the crew's careful preparation. But there was no going back to the same old reality.

Living *in Gratitude Mode* is like pressing that big red button. Gratitude is the key requirement for beginning your exciting journey of success. Continuing *in Gratitude Mode* assures you of positive changes along the way, nonstop changes that will amaze you. You know, changes for the better!

Chapter 4. A Personal Habit, or Personalizing a Habit..

I n a totally intuitive way, I began to incorporate gratitude into my daily routine a few years ago.

I used to just say "Thank God," when referring to an important achievement or emotion: "I feel fine, thank God," or "We achieved the sales goal, thank God." This is a very common habit in Latin America where we tend to be somewhat clingy to our traditions, often saying things without really thinking: that phrase was said by a family member or someone we admired.

More recently, and thanks to the process of change caused by my loss of vision, I began see and say things differently. I came across information that recommended gratitude practice as a tool to improve mental and emotional states.

So I started writing my blessings, not daily but frequently. I started to incorporate into my bedtime routine the process of feeling grateful for another day of light reaching my eyes, among other positives regarding my health. I genuinely felt that being able to see a new day was a great gift, especially when doctors had been predicting my blindness for years.

But my total confrontation with gratitude happened in 2011 when I settled permanently in the United States.

I will, of course, always be grateful for the opportunity to start my life over in this country. I also found myself surrounded by groups of wonderful people who encouraged various practices of gratitude that I'd been unaware of.

I am talking about people with visual difficulties and the team of volunteers and professionals of the Lighthouse of Broward.

The optimism and practical knowledge of my companions, plus the knowledge of helpful psychologists and counselors, joined to push me to investigate further and to practice gratitude regularly. By finding powerful genuine reasons to feel grateful, despite the limiting conditions that we may be facing in our lives.

After complete "life retraining," as I tend to call my time at the Lighthouse, and after beginning my studies to be certified as a personal coach, I discovered that what I intuitively perceived as beneficial had scientific bases in certain cases and, in others, strong statistical support.

Sharing Treasures

I've always loved sharing my findings with friends and family. If I find a good place to eat, or to take the kids, or to receive a service or professional consultation, I tell my inner circle of friends, using as much detail as possible, including address, contact information, rates and so on.

I could do no less with the discovered treasure that is gratitude. Not only is it a tool to be happier, more productive and healthier, as presented in Chapter Two, gratitude is a contribution, a boon to the general welfare. It's a state that nourishes he or she who experiences it while affecting those around him or her.

Gratitude is a mechanism of protection against anxiety, overwhelm and negativity. It permits us to connect with the positive, focusing our attention on what is good and positive, and analyze the negative from a perspective that permits us to overcome and transcend.

Making a Habit of Being Grateful

To incorporate gratitude as a habit and, in general, adopt any new habitual behavior, the desired action needs to be repeated in several sessions over several days.

Most of the specialists in human behavior have determined that in order to establish a habit you must repeat it for twenty-one consecutive days.

That's why many programs surrounding nutrition, meditation, and programs to stop a bad habit, operate in cycles of twenty-one days.

British psychologists recently determined that a habit is an individual process that can take between eighteen and sixty-six days. This is according to studies conducted on subjects of various ages and backgrounds attempting to develop habits, ranging from daily exercise to stopping procrastination.

This is why in the second part of this book I offer a total of sixty-three pages to use as a gratitude journal: three cycles of twenty-one days, with nearly the same number of pages for days as suggested by the later research.

In our case, to initiate the habit of gratitude, I recommend writing daily blessings. That is, make a written list of some of the reasons you have to feel grateful on this day in particular.

I recommend choosing a number between three and five and in your diary describe briefly these three to five things, situations or people for which you feel grateful.

As you describe them, try to identify the emotions or feelings that each causes; e.g., joy, peace, honor or satisfaction.

Try to identify a time of day when you feel comfortable journaling. It could be in the morning before beginning your daily routine, or before bedtime when you're relaxed. Writing in your diary is preparation for subsequent activities conducive to mental and physical states of focus, clarity and productivity.

Based on both scientific research and my own personal experience, I can say that a great time to write in your gratitude journal is before you go to sleep. In this way, you make a gradual transition from activity to rest, all the while establishing a positive mental attitude, inducing a relaxed and optimistic state that facilitates sleep.

This book contains enough space for you to start forming a habit of written gratitude in a format we hope you find practical, pleasant to the sight and inspiring.

As I mentioned earlier, there are enough pages for three cycles of twenty-one days. Once that period is over, you can continue in a journal or notebook, in traditional or electronic format, that's dedicated to gratitude.

I recommend using these pages because writing by hand has a beneficial effect. This intimate activity may be something we've not done since we were students. Handwriting activates mental and emotional connections that we use very little in our present day, so dominated by instant electronic transmission.

Writing in a gratitude journal will also allow us, in the future, to revisit pleasant memories and evaluate our progress toward our dream of an abundant life rich in well-being and success.

Customize the Habit

Each of us has a particular style of doing things. In the case of gratitude, you will most likely complete your journaling process in a completely unique way.

Still, I will share some additional suggestions so this activity can be even more special and rewarding for you:

- Try to keep this book alongside your gratitude journal, as well as pencil, pen, or any other element required for writing, such as glasses, pencil sharpener, eraser, or whatever;

- Create atmosphere; accompany journaling with some special element like a scented candle, soft music or simply total silence for deep contemplation;

- Place yourself in a relaxed but attentive mental state before beginning writing. To do this, take two or three deep breaths with your eyes closed;

- Feel free to read the section in "Winds of Inspiration" (later in this volume) corresponding to the current page. Or, if you prefer, read the section at the end of the exercise;

- Mentally review the moments, people and activities of that day for which you feel genuine gratitude. Choose the ones you will be talking about in the journal, then write them down;

- Remember to fill the appropriate spaces for time and date in your journal.

It is important to record the feelings produced by the gratitude you experience. Connecting with these emotions is a part of the healing process that gratitude initiates.

Sometimes these emotions can be intense, bringing you to a state of euphoria or tears. Don't be scared. Welcome these intense emotions and simply experience them.

In daily life, many times we are provided with moments or opportunities to experience emotions. In our modern world, everything happens quickly, one task followed by another in a sometimes senseless desire to produce more, do more, or prove more. At the end of the day, we're exhausted because, among other things, we do not allow ourselves to freely express our emotions.

When our bodies retain some vital element such as fluids, feces or even muscle tension, it can result in inflammation, discomfort and even disease.

What many people are unaware of is that trapped emotions, those not allowed to surface and flow freely, can also cause disease and pain, just as with retention of other bodily emanations.

Nowadays there is a renewed emphasis on the healthy channeling of emotions. This kind of release is sometimes used as additional therapy in the treatment of potentially fatal illnesses such as cancer.

I'm not a doctor but, as a mere measure of prevention, I recommend to my clients certain techniques that allow for a healthy flow of emotions. One of them is detailed in this book: the gratitude journal spoken of earlier.

As I've mentioned in previous chapters, the practice of gratitude can be extended to seemingly negative events in our lives, if we approach these circumstances as lessons. Under this premise, the emotions generated by gratitude can be a bit disconcerting at first. Let's look at an example.

Mary was the mother of two girls. So when her doctor

announced, in her fifth month of pregnancy, that she was expecting a baby boy, her joy was immense. But there was something else, another test that had to be taken. It certainly seemed that the baby had Down's Syndrome.

Mary was torn between gratitude, because she was impatient to meet her son, and fear due to her baby's condition. She cried a lot at first, questioned her faith, her luck, and even her family history and that of her husband.

It wasn't easy, but once Mary's baby was born, and as he grew into a child, she came to be genuinely grateful for him. The child made Mary learn about psychological and motor stimulation, which can be helpful with Down's. This therapy turned them into a family project to raise this special boy. The sisters became ever more patient and compassionate with their little brother, more so than they had been with each other. The parents were not only highly aware of the special child's emotional needs, but also that of the girls separately and as a couple.

Mary's emotions evolved from grief to acceptance, and finally into joy for every small success. It all ultimately became proactive, sharing her experience and information with other parents of children with Down's.

"Upon receiving the news," said Mary, "I had so many questions. And yet I never even considered an abortion. My husband and I are believers and consider life to be a gift from God: he gives and he takes it. We decided to prepare ourselves with information, talks and discussions on how to properly raise a child with Down's. I surrendered my sadness and distress to God in exchange for light and guidance in fulfilling the mission of raising my son and my girls."

Mary's spirituality was her gateway to gratitude. Everything her family or her new baby achieved was another reason to be grateful. "Despite feeling tired from all the work I had to do at home, and a bit sad from the curiosity or pity that my son received, at the end of the day I would write in my gratitude journal without fail. That helped me to stay strong and to learn from the very first years," Mary told me, lost in distant memories but with a smile and a knowing look in her eyes.

As shown by the above example, writing in a gratitude journal provides a mechanism for channeling emotions, allowing them to flow freely out of our bodily and mental systems, in the form of writing. This process also permits us to review our challenges, progress and achievements in overcoming circumstances that were initially perceived as adverse. This daily review not only allowed a learning and growth opportunity for Mary and her family, it also served as an example for you and me, as witnesses to the story of Mary and how gratitude can help in the process of acceptance.

Blocks and Obstacles

Like any process, the re-training of personal habits can present challenges during its development. In other words, we might feel apathetic toward, or too tired to, or too lacking in time for, journaling. Or we may feel so sad and frustrated that we do not feel grateful for anything.

Exactly as with exercising, or ceasing to eat flour products, or learning to use floss, forming a habit of gratitude can be hampered by old habits, in this case negative attitudes and defeatist thoughts.

To identify blockages and to overcome them, we must be familiar with the three elements that facilitate the formation of habits. Here we will focus on the habit of gratitude, more specifically the writing down of our daily blessings. Nevertheless, all these elements and recommendations for the formation of habits are valid for any type of habit.

However, it should be notes that there are differences in the requirement for the energy necessary to jog every morning versus writing every night in a journal. It is important to observe yourself and determine your particular characteristics when choosing an ideal time frame for a chosen activity.

To transform an occasional behavior into a habitual one, in other words, to form a habit, we all require three elements:

- **A Reminder:** an element that motivates us to begin the activity we want to establish as a habit.

In the present case, this book aims to become exactly such a reminder. I would thus recommend placing it in a special place where it can be easily accessed, to write in the journal section and to consult as a source of reference information.

- **A Routine:** the action we want to execute.

In your journal, jot down three to five situations, people or things for which you feel grateful that day. We want this act of writing to be easy and pleasant, hence the recommendations of creating an environment with candles or music and having everything needed nearby. I emphasize that it is important to record the feelings that each element recorded generates within you. It is extremely important to connect with the emotions of gratitude and experience them. If by any chance one draws your attention, you can analyze it in greater depth on another occasion, by yourself or with the support of a personal coach.

- **A Reward:** experience the benefits that the habit creates.

In the case of writing down daily blessings, the first benefit is to experience the flow of emotions generated by gratitude. Other immediate benefits might be that journaling facilitates sleep if you write just before going to sleep, or leads to a clear mental state if you do it at some moment of the day. Other benefits might show up at a more medium-term moment, depending on each person.

For a more comprehensive list of benefits, you can reread Chapter Two.

Bearing in mind these three elements (Reminder, Routine, Reward) will facilitate forming any new habit, but we must not abandon our process because a bump in the road. For instance, if we fail to write for one or two days or because we don't see any immediate results.

Repeating simple behaviors day by day is what reinforces a habit. The new behavior is built upon repetition. As one progresses, benefits become increasingly obvious.

Although number may seem not to apply to gratitude, try to quantify the benefits you notice. For example, are you experiencing more sleep, less anxiety about the unknown, more tasks performed during the day (greater productivity), or some other specific? You might try giving each blessing a numerical value, or place them in ranked order. Such quantifications allow us to value benefits or rewards more easily, making it easier to continue building the habit.

In conclusion, to prevent blockages in the development of a new habit, learn to facilitate your own process.

Create reminders for yourself. Place a positive note somewhere noticeable. Figure out the appropriate conditions and environment to facilitate your new routine. Obstacles can appear at any moment, in the form of oversight, fatigue, illness or a lag in motivation. Getting stalled is not defeat. Just start the routine back up as soon as you can. Remember, repetition is the key to forming any habit. Identify and quantify, whenever possible, the benefits or rewards received by the practice of your new habit.

In the case of gratitude, I assure you those benefits will be quite evident. And they will be abundant!

Chapter 5. My Personal Recipe for Gratitude (How to Use this Journal)

E verything happens for a reason. And sometimes those reasons are not clear until time has passed.

I truly believe that. Because many times in life I have gone through something, met someone or cast aside an idea, only to later realize that it was for the best. That something better or someone more fitted to the situation later shows up.

That's exactly what happened with this book.

I have always liked writing and have done so since I was a child, in the form of poems, songs, letters to friends (real and imaginary) and my beloved short stories. As a grown-up I began to write fiction and even spent four years researching and writing a novel that I have yet to finish.

But this book wrote itself. The idea emerged as a therapeutic fluidity of emotions and curiosities that lead me to remember and resume certain ideas, which meant reading, investigating and implementing new ideas. And finally, writing.

I have not abandoned my novel. It's simply that the book on gratitude took me by force, pushing me into action. And you hold in your hands the result.

A choice. It was one of many make in my life. And our choices shape the human experience.

Gratitude is a choice. As I was not currently writing my novel, I chose instead to write a book of mutual aid. I say mutual because this book, as I have said, has been a therapy for me, and I hope it may serve to inspire you. May you generate a more positive change in your own experience from my experience. And if, in addition, this book promotes a positive change to your surroundings, then you and I and everyone else benefit.

Living in Gratitude Mode, being grateful daily, has for me been a motivating element for moving forward and continuing to evolve and serve those around me. It has also been a way of channeling my anxiety and stress, as I can be grateful for the good in the parts that aren't going so well.

And I guess you understand. Because not everything in life is perfect, perfection is the enemy of the good, and of joy. Small achievements toward greater goals should not be seen as mediocre but leading toward a better and greater result.

I once wrote manually in my gratitude journal, in a small leather notebook (bound with the rubber band that has replaced the silk ribbon it originally came with, due to daily wear).

Manual exercise is wonderful. You can accompany your writings with doodles. I did: my personal emoticons at the time.

I no longer write on paper. It is too difficult, as I tend to write crookedly and my handwriting is awful. Also, it was not easy for me to later reread what I wrote, even with glasses.

So I adopted the laptop keyboard. A tablet frustrates me because I can never hit the right key. I waste time (as if that matters!). Actually, I like physical contact with the keyboard. I can write more words without errors, concentrating on the emotions and ideas. And it's just as effective for making my list of blessings, including my emotional responses, every day.

Some things appear in my journal repeatedly, especially my favorite people and core activities, like watching a new day appear or breathing.

On those days when I can't write, I am saying thanks mentally. Sometimes I extend it a bit more, like a meditation, because I can do this meditation lying in bed, before going to sleep, sitting, or even while brushing my teeth.

I think I've mentioned this enough times, but I truly recommend writing in the gratitude journal nightly before bedtime. That is how I do it, and I can vouch for the relaxing effect it has. Additionally, the thoughts and emotions of gratitude prepare the subconscious to express itself more freely through dreams.

While I cannot cite a psychological study or scientific paper that proves all of what I share from my personal experience, I can assure you that writing my blessings and being grateful for them before going to bed nightly, has allowed me to sleep well and without nightmares for many years. At least twelve years up to now.

Sometimes I have tried lighting scented candle (the fragrance recommended for relaxation is lavender); I have also tried playing relaxing music; I've even prayed before and after writing in my gratitude journal. I currently prefer silence. I just listen to the sounds from the computer that allow me to write and correct my spelling, just as I'm doing now in writing this book.

So did my daily practice ritual evolve. And yours very probably will, as well, adapting to your circumstances and preferences. That is what makes a real habit: a routine that integrates gently into your day-to-day and evolves along with you.

Action!

Get ready to write your daily blessings. Here is the step-by-step:

1. **Prepare your environment:** locate the place where you feel most comfortable to write. Put in place your book, notebook, pencil or pen, light, glasses, all supplies required;

2. **Mental preparation:** focus your attention in a relaxed manner; take three deep breaths, through the nose with eyes closed;

3. **Give the moment special attention:** if you'd like, enrich your experience with scents or sounds that facilitate focus and relaxation. You can read the Winds of Inspiration section before writing;

4. **Stick to your routine:** choose a number of blessings to be grateful for. I suggest three to five. Name them, meaning, say what you are grateful for. Now describe them in your journal. This amounts to explaining why you're grateful today. Do it, including the emotions and sensations of gratitude these things inspire in you;

5. **Remember to write down the date and time of the exercise.** This will allow you to check your commitment to the habit, and help you determine the most favorable time for practice.

Regularly review your notes, note the changes that practicing gratitude have caused in your life. This is the reward of wellness that gratitude offers.

I can only be grateful to you for allowing me to share these ideas and suggestions with you. I reiterate my sincere desire for your well-being, and that living in Gratitude Mode allows a happier existence and many abundant blessings.

PART TWO: *Gratitude Journal*

Day 1: / /

Time:

Winds of Inspiration

True gratitude emerges spontaneously. Our own actions must reflect what we feel, what we consider positive and appropriate. The simple fact that we can express ourselves freely must be our reward.

"Act with kindness, but do not expect gratitude."

Confucius (551-479a.C.). Chinese Philosopher.

Gifts of the Day

_____

_____

_____

_____

_____

_____

_____

Day 2:   /   /

Time:

Winds of Inspiration

Gratitude is a great ally for experiencing happiness and joy. Turn it into your confidant. Speak to it when you cannot directly thank the person you would like to thank. But most of all, access your full powers of expressing it.

Gifts of the Day

_____
_____
_____
_____
_____
_____
_____
_____
_____
_____

Day 3:   /   /

Time:

Winds of Inspiration

Gratitude is like a muscle that develops and strengthens with use. Even if you think you lack gratitude, practice will enable the feeling to appear.

Gifts of the Day

_____

_____

_____

_____

_____

_____

_____

_____

_____

_____

_____

_____

Day 4: / /

Time:

Winds of Inspiration

When fatigue saps your strength, thank it for having been there during your achievement.

Many times we focus on the difficulties caused by a life filled with activities, people we care about, and projects. We forget that just having so much to do, and having the opportunity to do it all, is a blessing to be grateful for.

Gifts of the Day

_____
_____
_____
_____
_____
_____
_____
_____

Day 5: / /

Time:

Winds of Inspiration

"Let us arise and be grateful because if we have not learned much,
at least we have learned that. And if we have not learned that, at least
we are not sick. And if we are sick, at least we are not dead. So today,
let us all be grateful."

Buddha

Gifts of the Day

_____
_____
_____
_____
_____
_____
_____
_____
_____
_____

Day 6: / /

Time:

Winds of Inspiration

Gratitude opens the door to the fullness of existence. It transforms what we have into more than enough. It turns denial into acceptance, chaos into order, and confusion into clarity. A meal becomes a banquet, a house becomes a home, a stranger becomes a friend.

Gifts of the Day

_____

_____

_____

_____

_____

_____

_____

_____

_____

_____

_____

Day 7: __/__/__

Time:

Winds of Inspiration

Gratitude gives meaning to our past, brings peace to our present, and provides optimism to our future.

Gifts of the Day

_____
_____
_____
_____
_____
_____
_____
_____
_____
_____
_____
_____

Day 8: ___/___/___

Time:

Winds of Inspiration

Gratitude is the main chord in the symphony of friendship.

Gifts of the Day

_____
_____
_____
_____
_____
_____
_____
_____
_____
_____
_____
_____
_____
_____

Day 9: ___/___/___

Time:

Winds of Inspiration

An ingrate is one who does not recognize that gratitude is a gift to oneself.

Gifts of the Day

_____

_____

_____

_____

_____

_____

_____

_____

_____

_____

_____

_____

Day 10:   /   /

Time:

Winds of Inspiration

Some people think that prayer is only for the religious. They confuse spirituality with religiosity. But if the only prayer you say in your life is: "Thank you," that will be more than enough as a spiritual practice.

Gifts of the Day

_____

_____

_____

_____

_____

_____

_____

_____

_____

_____

Day 11: / /

Time:

Winds of Inspiration

According to Aristotle, gratitude ages quickly. *Is that why one should express it whenever possible?* Sometimes people forget to refresh their own memories, as well as others'.

Gifts of the Day

Day 12:   /   /

Time:

Winds of Inspiration

Those filled with pride rarely feel grateful because they never feel that they get everything they deserve.

Gifts of the Day

_____

_____

_____

_____

_____

_____

_____

_____

_____

_____

_____

_____

Day 13:   /   /

Time:

Winds of Inspiration

"He who does not give thanks for a little, will not give thanks for a lot."

Estonian Proverb

Gifts of the Day

_____
_____
_____
_____
_____
_____
_____
_____
_____
_____
_____
_____

Day 14:   /   /

Time:

Winds of Inspiration

You can be taught to say *thanks* but not to be grateful. Gratitude is a feeling that grows with practice.

Gifts of the Day

_____

_____

_____

_____

_____

_____

_____

_____

_____

_____

_____

_____

_____

Day 15:   /   /

Time:

Winds of Inspiration

Let us make gratitude our daily offering and evening devotion to God.

Gifts of the Day

_____

_____

_____

_____

_____

_____

_____

_____

_____

_____

_____

_____

_____

Day 16: / /

Time:

Winds of Inspiration

We always have something for which to be grateful.

Gifts of the Day

_____
_____
_____
_____
_____
_____
_____
_____
_____
_____
_____
_____
_____
_____

Day 17: __/__/__

Time:

Winds of Inspiration

Stopping to observe what we have, giving thanks for it—these are the initial steps to increased abundance.

Gifts of the Day

_____

_____

_____

_____

_____

_____

_____

_____

_____

_____

_____

_____

Day 18:   /   /

Time:

Winds of Inspiration

Sometimes it is difficult to be grateful because we cannot immediately see the results of our practice. Distancing ourselves is not only a matter of space but also of passion.

Gifts of the Day

_____
_____
_____
_____
_____
_____
_____
_____
_____
_____
_____

Jeanette Salvatierra

114

Day 19: / /

Time:

Winds of Inspiration

Being grateful is like watering the seeds of our well-being.

Gifts of the Day

Day 20:   /   /

Time:

Winds of Inspiration

A grateful attitude makes possible humility, which is so important when serving others.

Gifts of the Day

_____
_____
_____
_____
_____
_____
_____
_____
_____
_____
_____
_____

Day 21: / /

Time:

Winds of Inspiration

"He who receives a benefit, should never forget it; whoever provides it, should never remember."

Pierre Charron (1541-1603) French Philosopher

Gifts of the Day

_____

_____

_____

_____

_____

_____

_____

_____

_____

_____

_____

_____

Day 22:   /   /

Time:

Winds of Inspiration

"Hope has a good memory. Gratitude has a very poor one."

Baltasar Gracian (1601 – 1658) Spanish philosopher and writer

Gifts of the Day

_____
_____
_____
_____
_____
_____
_____
_____
_____
_____
_____
_____
_____

Day 23:   /   /

Time:

Winds of Inspiration

Perhaps more difficult than striving to constantly be grateful, is receiving the sincere gratitude of others. In such a case, the eloquence of silence and a smile is often enough.

Gifts of the Day

_____
_____
_____
_____
_____
_____
_____
_____
_____
_____
_____

Day 24:   /   /

Time:

Winds of Inspiration

We feel affection and gratitude for our friends, let us recognize them as providential to our human experience.

Gifts of the Day

_____

_____

_____

_____

_____

_____

_____

_____

_____

_____

_____

_____

_____

_____

Day 25: / /

Time:

Winds of Inspiration

"Do not throw garbage into the well you drink from."

Talmut.

Due to changes in circumstances, we may find ourselves unhappy about something or with someone to whom we owe a debt of gratitude. Let us not fog our memory with resentment but refresh our gratitude in silence.

Gifts of the Day

Day 26:   /   /

Time:

Winds of Inspiration

We can choose many ways to express our gratitude. But the most eloquent way is to live honoring that which we're grateful for.

Gifts of the Day

_____

_____

_____

_____

_____

_____

_____

_____

_____

_____

_____

_____

_____

Day 27: / /

Time:

Winds of Inspiration

"Gratitude is the memory of the heart."

Lao Tzu (570 - 490 B.C.) Taoist Philosopher

Gifts of the Day

_____

_____

_____

_____

_____

_____

_____

_____

_____

_____

_____

Day 28:   /   /

Time:

Winds of Inspiration

"No worthy man will ask that you thank him for anything that
costs him nothing."

Terence (circa 185 - 159 B.C.) Latin playwright

Gifts of the Day

_____
_____
_____
_____
_____
_____
_____
_____
_____
_____
_____
_____

Day 29:   /   /

Time:

Winds of Inspiration

He who is not grateful, probably never deserved what he received.

Gifts of the Day

_____
_____
_____
_____
_____
_____
_____
_____
_____
_____
_____
_____
_____

Day 30:   /   /

Time:

Winds of Inspiration

"Gratitude is the main part of a good man."

Francisco de Quevedo (1580-1645) Spanish writer

Gifts of the Day

_____

_____

_____

_____

_____

_____

_____

_____

_____

_____

_____

_____

Day 31:   /   /

Time:

Winds of Inspiration

After receiving a benefit, he who is grateful not only recognizes his benefactor directly, but also everyone who made it possible for the benefactor to give help.

Gifts of the Day

_____

_____

_____

_____

_____

_____

_____

_____

_____

_____

_____

_____

Day 32:   /   /

Time:

Winds of Inspiration

Gratitude makes us more appealing to others—and is cheaper and less painful than surgery.

Gifts of the Day

_____

_____

_____

_____

_____

_____

_____

_____

_____

_____

_____

_____

Day 33:   /   /

Time:

Winds of Inspiration

When I remember all those who have supported me, loved me, helped me, even criticized me in my life, my gratitude is summarized in wishing they receive double the benefits I have received from them.

Gifts of the Day

_____

_____

_____

_____

_____

_____

_____

_____

_____

_____

Day 34:   /   /

Time:

Winds of Inspiration

Great teachers are not great because of their greatness but because of their wisdom and gratitude toward those who taught them what they now teach us.

Gifts of the Day

Day 35: / /

Time:

Winds of Inspiration

Today I am grateful to gratitude for the calm that it brings to my life when I feel it, and for the love I continue to receive when I express it.

Gifts of the Day

_____
_____
_____
_____
_____
_____
_____
_____
_____
_____
_____

Day 36: / /

Time:

Winds of Inspiration

The practice of gratitude magnifies the benefits of other spiritual practices, like meditation and charity. What are your favorite spiritual practices?

Gifts of the Day

_____
_____
_____
_____
_____
_____
_____
_____
_____
_____

Day 37: / /

Time:

Winds of Inspiration

"There are so many gifts / unopened since your birth / that are so many hand-made presents / that have been sent to you by God. / The Beloved does not mind repeating, / 'Everything I have belongs to you, too."

Hafiz, Sufi poet

Gifts of the Day

_____

_____

_____

_____

_____

_____

_____

_____

_____

_____

Day 38:   /   /

Time:

Winds of Inspiration

It's time to gracefully bow down to all the gifts of beauty, joy, love, laughter and happiness with which divinity has adorned our existence.

Gifts of the Day

_____
_____
_____
_____
_____
_____
_____
_____
_____
_____

Day 39: / /

Time:

Winds of Inspiration

"There is so much greatness of mind in acknowledging a good action, and then doing one."

Seneca (4 B.C. – 65 B.C.) Roman playwright/philosopher

Gifts of the Day

_____

_____

_____

_____

_____

_____

_____

_____

_____

_____

_____

Day 40:   /   /

Time:

Winds of Inspiration

"I will praise you, Lord, with all my heart; / before the "gods" I will sing your praise. / I will bow down toward your holy temple / and will praise your name / for your unfailing love and your faithfulness, / for you have so exalted your solemn decree / that it surpasses your fame."

Psalm 138

Gifts of the Day

_____

_____

_____

_____

_____

_____

_____

_____

_____

Day 41:   /   /

Time:

Winds of Inspiration

Celebrate all that you have and what you want most in your life. Gratitude for abundance multiplies your gifts and your joy.

Gifts of the Day

_____

_____

_____

_____

_____

_____

_____

_____

_____

_____

_____

_____

Day 42:   /   /

Time:

Winds of Inspiration

"There is no excess in the world more beautiful than gratitude."

Jewish Proverb

Gifts of the Day

_____

_____

_____

_____

_____

_____

_____

_____

_____

_____

_____

_____

Day 43:   /   /

Time:

Winds of Inspiration

If feeling and expressing love, loyalty and gratitude, requires having a soul, then many animals possess an enormous soul.

Gifts of the Day

_____

_____

_____

_____

_____

_____

_____

_____

_____

_____

_____

_____

_____

Day 44:   /   /

Time:

Winds of Inspiration

No matter how bright or stormy the day I'm living today, I keep a grateful attitude. If I insist on seeing the day as gloomy, I will try to remember tomorrow is a new day.

Gifts of the Day

_____

_____

_____

_____

_____

_____

_____

_____

_____

_____

_____

_____

Day 45: / /

Time:

Winds of Inspiration

"Cultivate the habit of being grateful for every good thing that comes to you, and of giving thanks continuously. And because all things have contributed to your advancement, you should include all things in your gratitude."

Ralph Waldo Emerson (1803-1882) American essayist/poet/speaker

Gifts of the Day

_____

_____

_____

_____

_____

_____

_____

_____

_____

Day 46:   /   /

Time:

Winds of Inspiration

"When we were children we were grateful to those who filled our stockings at Christmastime. Why are we not grateful to God for filling our stockings with legs?"

Gilbert Keith Chesterton (1874-1936) British Writer

Gifts of the Day

_____

_____

_____

_____

_____

_____

_____

_____

_____

_____

Day 47: / /

Time:

Winds of Inspiration

"Gratitude, like certain flowers, does not stem from high places but is the greenest rising from the good soil of humility."

José Martí (1853 - 1895) Cuban writer

Gifts of the Day

_____

_____

_____

_____

_____

_____

_____

_____

_____

_____

_____

_____

Day 48:   /   /

Time:

Winds of Inspiration

"Love is the greatest gift that God could have given us. If you do not have it, look for it; if you have it, take care of it for you are a lucky person."

Anonymous

Gifts of the Day

_____

_____

_____

_____

_____

_____

_____

_____

_____

_____

_____

Day 49: / /

Time:

Winds of Inspiration

"There is no more necessary duty than to give thanks."

Marcus Tullius Cicero (106-43 B.C.) Roman philosopher

Gifts of the Day

_____

_____

_____

_____

_____

_____

_____

_____

_____

_____

_____

_____

175

Day 50: / /

Time:

Winds of Inspiration

"The oyster becomes sick because it carries the pearl, and you thank heaven that it ennobles you with pain."

Friedrich Rückert (1788 - 1866) German Professor of Oriental Languages

Gifts of the Day

_____
_____
_____
_____
_____
_____
_____
_____
_____
_____
_____

Day 51: / /

Time:

Winds of Inspiration

"Rejoice always, pray continually, give thanks in all circumstances;
for this is God's will for you (...) BE GRATEFUL FOR IT ALL..."

Thessalonians 5:16-18

Gifts of the Day

Day 52: / /

Time:

Winds of Inspiration

"And to all those who threw stones at me, thanks! Because with them I built the walls of the house where my soul lives today."

Anonymous

Gifts of the Day

_____

_____

_____

_____

_____

_____

_____

_____

_____

_____

Day 53:   /   /

Time:

Winds of Inspiration

Friendship is the garden we water with gratitude so that it may flourish for life.

Gifts of the Day

_____
_____
_____
_____
_____
_____
_____
_____
_____
_____
_____
_____
_____

Day 54:   /   /

Time:

Winds of Inspiration

"If I could explain how much I owe my great predecessors and contemporaries, I wouldn't possess much property."

Johann Wolfgang von Goethe (1749 - 1832) German writer

Gifts of the Day

_____
_____
_____
_____
_____
_____
_____
_____
_____
_____
_____

Day 55:   /   /

Time:

Winds of Inspiration

"Gratitude is the fairest blossom which springs from the soul."

Henry Ward Beecher (1813-1887) American politician

Gifts of the Day

_____

_____

_____

_____

_____

_____

_____

_____

_____

_____

_____

_____

_____

_____

Day 56: / /

Time:

Winds of Inspiration

I am *grateful* for who I am.

Gifts of the Day

_____

_____

_____

_____

_____

_____

_____

_____

_____

_____

_____

_____

Day 57:   /   /

Time:

Winds of Inspiration

You experience so much joy in serving others, you want to thank them.

Gifts of the Day

_____
_____
_____
_____
_____
_____
_____
_____
_____
_____
_____
_____
_____

Day 58:   /   /

Time:

Winds of Inspiration

"Let us be grateful to people who make us happy, they are the charming gardeners who make our souls blossom."

Will Rogers (1879 - 1935) American writer

Gifts of the Day

_____

_____

_____

_____

_____

_____

_____

_____

_____

_____

_____

_____

Day 59:   /   /

Time:

Winds of Inspiration

"No, it is I who am grateful to you ... for having found her...."

Fyodor Mikhailovich Dostoevsky (1821 - 1881) Russian novelist

Gifts of the Day

_____
_____
_____
_____
_____
_____
_____
_____
_____
_____
_____
_____
_____

Day 60:   /   /

Time:

Winds of Inspiration

"He who does not appreciate a little favor will not appreciate a big one".

Muhammad (570-632) Islamic prophet

Gifts of the Day

_____

_____

_____

_____

_____

_____

_____

_____

_____

_____

_____

Day 61:   /   /

Time:

Winds of Inspiration

We are often not grateful for something really valuable, because we are used to, thus insensitive to, its presence in our lives.

Gifts of the Day

_____

_____

_____

_____

_____

_____

_____

_____

_____

_____

_____

_____

Day 62: / /

Time:

Winds of Inspiration

When the choice we make is to be grateful for our circumstances, whatever they may be, we recharge our batteries with positive energy to implement actions that will enable us to overcome the situation.

Gifts of the Day

_____
_____
_____
_____
_____
_____
_____
_____
_____
_____
_____

Day 63:   /   /

Time:

Winds of Inspiration

Love is meant to be shared. If love inspires gratitude, share that feeling with others. It will be worth it.

Gifts of the Day

_____

_____

_____

_____

_____

_____

_____

_____

_____

_____

_____

_____

PART THREE: *The Legacy of the Gratitude Journal*

Chapter 1. Expanding on the Rewards

I hope that by now writing in your gratitude journal has manifested increased abundance and well-being in your life.

The human experience is a journey, a transition from womb to ultimate reintegration with our higher selves. This journey has been compared by writers and poets to a voyage by sea, air or land.

For me, it is a path, an earthly path on a planet of soil and water. We began our paths the second we took our first breath, followed by the cry we let out when we abandoned a warm, loving womb.

Before we even know how to walk, we are already on the path. With great joy, lots of curiosity and a hint of fear, but with the support of parents and caregivers, friends and teachers. And always, under the guidance of our higher self.

Sometimes we are courageous. Sometimes we're cautious. We move along almost effortlessly, even when time seems to slow us down.

Sometimes we have to cross a body of water, like a river or an ocean, because we cannot continue growing and learning in our former environment.

We must, therefore, prepare to cross, to find the appropriate boat and provisions to cross that body of water, to begin to grow, to learn and live with a new quality of life.

Every step, every journey, leads to new areas, and we'll likely need to make inner changes to adapt to our new conditions. The change is accomplished by maintaining your values and being more flexible with your ideas.

We are required to present ourselves to our new neighbors or authorities, All the while observing our circumstances, our emotions and our wishes to transform. Most of all, we need to appreciate what we have, decanting the personal essence of our being through gratitude.

This is how gratitude is your passport to a better life, one more full and abundant in blessings.

Moving along a path begins with gratitude for, first of all, the opportunity to start over, to bring forth who we are and what we can share with a new human group. We can feel grateful for potential new achievements, new friendships and affections, and for our new home and community.

Gratitude connects us with abundance, with the infinite potential of the universe, and with our well-being and what we can potentially create in our environment through work and service.

Developing the capacity for gratitude and making it a habit, facilitates our fitting into our new context of physical and human relations.

From its first manifestation, the cosmic passport of gratitude facilitates finding our comfort zone, our new reality and new emotions in our new circumstances.

Every path has its difficulties. Even the path most often taken has generated upset, uneasiness, doubt and anxiety. To be grateful for the opportunity of being able to walk the path and all its potholes, opens our minds and spirits to new possibilities, solutions and opportunities for personal development.

We continue along our path confident that we are prepared and equipped to achieve our dreams and goals.

Expanding on New Habits through the Seven Questions

When we practice gratitude, the first things we may notice are various aspects of our life experience, choosing those that impact us most decisively. The importance of each aspect is very personal. We may be grateful for something today that won't be a part of our written list of blessings tomorrow or the day after. But it will always remain in our experience, in our memories, and in our journals.

Once we identify what we are grateful for, the second step is to identify why.

The reason for our gratitude goes back to our personal values and goals. Maybe it's a means, a step in achieving a complex goal, or it can be a person, a group or a team of people who provide for us in some area of our existence.

The third step is to observe the emotions that are generated in our being when we are grateful for that person or thing. By recognizing our emotions and feelings, we deepen the experience of gratitude, creating more complete and indelible memories.

If you have followed the recommendations in this book, including the daily journaling, you have obtained your passport to abundance and well-being. The positive memories, a product of the above three steps, form the basis for achieving the benefits of gratitude in the long-term.

As with all passports, gratitude allows us to expand our path onto new roads. It allows us to travel to new, interesting and useful places, whether for business or pleasure. Gratitude expands our capacity to appreciate new things, people and experiences.

However, a passport has to be used. In the case of gratitude, using the passport means trying out these tools and analyzing their benefits in our lives.

Deepening our experience with gratitude, accelerates and enriches the process of personal growth.

How do we deeper gratitude?

The approach proposed by this book is based on seven questions. Some apply to specific areas for which we are most grateful, and other questions analyze the practice of gratitude in general.

How has your life changed since experiencing gratitude?

The practice or habit of gratitude can drive you to many varied changes, ranging from a simple modification of your daily routine to beginning other practices for personal growth, such as exercise, meditation, improving communication skills, or beginning a savings or investment program.

It is also possible that the practice of gratitude causes you to abandon some other activity or relationship with certain people, or ideas that previously seemed appropriate and attractive but no longer feel the same. By enhancing certain things and diminishing others, the practice of gratitude modifies our perceptions and, so, our behaviors and relationships.

For example, in my personal experience, gratitude has helped me become more disciplined. By analyzing which would be the best time to write in my journal, I was able to reconsider and prioritize my activities. Identifying a person or activity for which to be grateful, encourages me to spend more time with that person, or doing that activity.

Do you think that gratitude has transformed your quality of life?

As we explained in Chapter Two, gratitude offers benefits to those who practice it in various areas of their life, from one's own personality, to his or her work relationships, health and emotions.

When considering something in depth, identify the benefit it provides.

Observing what we receive when being grateful for something, we look for beneficial patterns in our lives.

So, for example, when thanking a colleague or subordinate at work, we are strengthening our professional links and making for a more pleasant work environment. If writing in our journal at a certain time, or expressing our gratitude to someone personally, facilitates a subsequent activity, like sleep or digestion; repeat that same act of gratitude the next day, and obtain the same benefits.

These new patterns reinforce our efforts, and we build upon gratitude as a habit.

Additionally, experiencing the benefits of gratitude transforms and elevates our quality of life in general, because these patterns often have a beneficial impact on multiple aspects of our lives. For example, better work relationships can improve productivity and economic success. Improved physical and mental health can allow us to be more emotionally stable and better provide for our families and relationships.

Basically, identifying the specific benefit that gratitude brings to our lives, makes us more conscious of the transformation occurring in our quality of life through our practice of gratitude.

Have you modified your mental clarity, creativity and/or productivity, as a result of your gratitude practice? In what way?

To answer this question, I recommend mentally going over the activities of several days or weeks, and observing your expressions of creativity, any changes in productivity, and the moments of mental clarity you may have experienced.

If possible, compare these observations with comments recorded previously, before or early into your practice of gratitude.

These changes constitute new areas for which to be grateful, and I recommend writing them down in your journal. This will allow you to document your progress in productivity, creativity and clarity, which will serve you as a basis for further analysis and research.

In what way has gratitude impacted your relationships?

When the aspect we are grateful for is a personal or professional relationship, this answer may seem obvious.

But what's interesting is that gratitude in one aspect of our lives may impact upon other areas, and a common result of gratitude practice in general is better relationships with others.

For example:

- Gratitude for having received an important project because it may mean a chance of a family vacation at the end of the year, which will strengthen relationships with our partner, children and/or parents;

- Gratitude for a healthy diagnosis for a close relative of a colleague, which may lead to greater harmony and joy in the work team, possibly reducing the time required to complete an important project.

The intent of this question is to walk us through the ramifications of our gratitude as it relates to relationships, both personal and professional, and even on the level of community.

Has gratitude had a ripple effect on your environment?

This question invites you to explore beyond your mind and body, and consider the broader impact of your gratitude.

First, observe your environment, your friends, family and colleagues. Casually ask them if they have noticed any change in you, or whether they have felt a shift in their feelings about you.

Sometimes our own perception or intuition is enough for us to identify the impact the practice of gratitude has had on our environment. Other peoples' validations of these perceptions are not required, but they may bring us closer to a complete understanding, as well as demonstrating our interest in the feelings of others.

How has gratitude changed your perception of your role in the world?

Congratulations! Now that you have begun the practice of gratitude, your level of consciousness has already increased.

By that, I mean you have thoughtfully observed the events and people in your life, selecting those for which you are grateful, careful to examine each of your thoughts. This can only help you recognize the effects of certain people, activities and thoughts, on your body and your life.

You can more easily recognize that which troubles you, that

which is you are passionate about, and what you feel indifferent about.

This awareness not only enables you to strengthen your positive habits and activities, but also facilitates identification of new activities and roles, and gives you greater satisfaction and meaning in your life.

Has gratitude strengthened your spirituality?

This is perhaps the question that holds the greatest depth. To facilitate this kind of analysis and reflection, take a pause in your reading, close your eyes, and take three deep breaths through your nose.

Spirituality has different expressions in different people. As individual as the expression of the self, spirituality has many faces.

Spirituality is awareness that we are more than body and mind. It's nurturing win-win relationships. Spirituality can be working for what we are passionate about, which, hopefully, is just as useful to others as it is to us. These are just a few examples of spiritual practice that we may not be aware of.

Take a moment to reflect on the following aspects of a spiritual life, and try to determine what particular expressions they have taken in your life:

- Your awareness of the mind-body--spirit triad;
- Your passion for an activity, whether paid or not;
- How this activity enables you to speak and interact with other people, or with nature;
- How your activity impacts the lives of others, helping them to be healthier happier, or in some way better.

There are other expressions of spirituality that are well-known and apply to people we typically perceive as spiritual. These practices, too, require review and reflection, and to be analyzed through the lens of gratitude. Below are some other spiritual practices than can, and may have, deepened your life:

- **Prayer:** perhaps the traditional recitation of prayers or, better, spontaneous conversation, in your own words, with your higher self or God;

- **Meditation,** contemplation or some other practice of stillness and listening;

- **Charity:** solidarity with people in need through participation in individual or collective efforts to help out;

- **Faith:** trust in God without evidence or physical demonstrations;

- **Virtue:** developing such qualities as patience, compassion, transparency, courage, hospitality, respect, confidence in yourself, industriousness, tolerance, loyalty or perseverance.

By paying attention to ourselves and our environment, we can identify attitudes and positions that are "little to non-" spiritual. Identifying those is the first step to eradicating the negative from our lives, or avoiding their negative influences:

- Materialism;

- Envy;

- Dishonesty (the desire to take unfair advantage of people or situations.)

I will not dwell on this list because its energy is low in frequency and not the route to well-being. But I think you get the idea.

It's very common for people who practice gratitude to recognize those who do not practice it. I can tell you from personal experience, it can even feel uncomfortable when you're with a person who has something to be grateful for but isn't. I suggest silently offering gratitude for them. And if you feel a level of trust and confidence with the other person, you might invite him or her to be grateful.

If, or rather when, you follow these guidelines, you will become a living testimony of the benefits of practicing gratitude. Do not be afraid to draw attention to your gratitude, or to have others comment on it. Sharing your spiritual practice is part of the responsibility of being alive and connected to other living beings.

The many benefits of gratitude are freely available. This is a light and a power that is never-ending, expanding more and more with use and expression.

One Last Thing...

Thanks again for letting me come along, through these pages we've shared, on your journey toward personal well-being and abundance. May the blessings of living In Gratitude Mode multiply within you and your loved ones, and through you to the rest of the world.

Jeanette Salvatierra-Barrios.

BIBLIOGRAPHY

Emmons, Robert A., McCullough, Michael E. 2003: "Counting Blessings Versus Burdens: An Experimental Investigation of Subjective Well-Being in Daily Life." *Journal of Personality and Social Psychology*, Vol. 84(2), Feb, pp. 377-89.

DeAngelis, Tori. 2004: "Consumerism and its Discontents." June, Vol. 35, No. 6.

DOI Kennon, Sheldon M., Lyubomirsky, Sonja B. 2006: "How to Increase and Sustain Positive Emotion: The Effects of Expressing Gratitude and Visualizing Our Best Possible Selves." *The Journal of Positive Psychology*, Vol. 1, Issue 2, Special Issue: Positive Emotions, pp. 73-82.

Gottman, John, Schwartz-Gottman, Julie. 2015: *Seven Principles to Make Marriage Work*. The Gottman Institute, various seminars, books and videos.

Gottman, J.M., Gottman, J.S. 2008: "Gottman Method Couple Therapy." In *Gurmna, A.S., Clinical Handbook of Couple Therapy*, Chapter 5, pp. 138-66.

Grant, A.M., et al. 2010: "A Little Thanks Goes a Long Way: Explaining Why Gratitude Expressions Motivate Prosocial Behavior." *Journal of Personality and Social Psychology*, June. Vol. 98, No. 6, pp. 946-55.

Lambert, N.M., et al. 2011: "Expressing Gratitude to a Partner Leads to More Relationship Maintenance Behavior." *Emotion,* Feb., Vol. 11, No. 1, pp. 52-60.

Sansone, R.A., et al. 2010: "Gratitude and Well Being: The Benefits of Appreciation." *Psychiatry,* Nov., Vol. 7, No. 11, pp. 18-22.

Seligman, M.E.P., et al. 2005: "Empirical Validation of Interventions." *American Psychologist,* July-Aug. Vol. 60, No. 1, pp. 410-21.

Watkins, Philip C.; Woodward, Kathrane; Stone, Tamara; Kolts, Russell L. 2003: "Gratitude and Happiness: Development of a Measure of Gratitude and Relationships with Subjective Well-Being." *Social Behavior and Personality,* Vol. 31, Number 5, pp. 431-51(21)

Wood, Alex M.; Maltby, John; Gillett, Raphael; Linley, Alex; Joseph, Stephen. 2008: "The Role of Gratitude in the Development of Social Support, Stress and Depression: Two Longitudinal Studies." *Journal of Research on Personality,* August, Vol. 42, Issue 4, pp. 854-71.

www.ingramcontent.com/pod-product-compliance
Lightning Source LLC
LaVergne TN
LVHW041215080426
835508LV00011B/961